WEATHER

Also by Lee Bennett Hopkins

I Can Read Books®

Surprises

More Surprises

Questions

Picture Books

Best Friends

By Myself

Good Books, Good Times!

Morning, Noon and Nighttime, Too

The Sky Is Full of Song

Books for Middle Grades

Mama and Her Boys

Click, Rumble, Roar

Professional Reading

Pass the Poetry, Please!

Let Them Be Themselves

WEATHER

Poems selected by

Lee Bennett Hopkins

Pictures by **Melanie Hall**

HarperCollins_Publishers_

I Can Read Book is a registered trademark of
HarperCollins Publishers.

WEATHER
Text copyright © 1994 by Lee Bennett Hopkins
Illustrations copyright © 1994 by Melanie Hall
Printed in the U.S.A. All rights reserved.

Library of Congress Cataloging-in-Publication Data
Hopkins, Lee Bennett.
    Weather / poems selected by Lee Bennett Hopkins ; pictures by
Melanie Hall.
        p.   cm. — (An I can read book)
    Summary: A collection of poems describing various weather
conditions, by authors such as Christina G. Rossetti, Myra Cohn
Livingston, and Aileen Fisher.
    ISBN 0-06-021463-5. — ISBN 0-06-021462-7 (lib. bdg.)
    1. Weather—Juvenile poetry.   2. Children's poetry, American.
3. Children's poetry, English.   [1. Weather—Poetry.
2. American poetry—Collections.   3. English poetry—Collections.]
I. Hall, Melanie, ill.   II. Title.   III. Series.
PS595.W38H66   1994   92-14913
811.008'036—dc20   CIP
                                                  AC

1   2   3   4   5   6   7   8   9   10 ❖
First Edition

To my great-niece
   ToniLynn Christine Yavorski
   In all kinds of weather!

                 LBH

To my teacher
   Fred Brenner
   with great affection

                 MWH

ACKNOWLEDGMENTS

Every effort has been made to trace the ownership of all copyrighted material and to secure the necessary permissions to reprint these selections. In the event of any question arising as to the use of any material, the editor and the publisher, while expressing regret for any inadvertent error, will be happy to make the necessary correction in future printings.

Thanks are due to the following for permission to reprint the copyrighted materials listed below:

Curtis Brown, Ltd., for "A Week of Weather" by Lee Bennett Hopkins. Copyright © 1974 by Lee Bennett Hopkins; "Thunder" by Lee Bennett Hopkins. Copyright © 1994 by Lee Bennett Hopkins. Used by permission of Curtis Brown, Ltd.

Farrar, Straus & Giroux, Inc., for "Sun" from *Small Poems* by Valerie Worth. Copyright © 1972 by Valerie Worth. Reprinted by permission of Farrar, Straus & Giroux, Inc.

Lillian M. Fisher for "Weather Together." Used by permission of the author, who controls all rights.

Isabel Joshlin Glaser for "On A Summer Day." Used by permission of the author, who controls all rights.

Harcourt Brace Jovanovich, Inc., for "Fog" from *Chicago Poems* by Carl Sandburg, copyright 1916 by Holt, Rinehart and Wintson, Inc., and renewed 1944 by Carl Sandburg; "Grayness" from *Everything Glistens and Everything Sings* by Charlotte Zolotow. Copyright © 1987 by Charlotte Zolotow. Both reprinted by permission of Harcourt Brace Jovanovich, Inc.

HarperCollins Publishers for "Looking Out the Window" from *Out in the Dark and Daylight* by Aileen Fisher. Copyright © 1980 by Aileen Fisher; "Icicles" from *Cold Stars and Fireflies: Poems of the Four Seasons* by Barbara Juster Esbensen. Copyright © 1984 by Barbara Juster Esbensen. Both reprinted by permission of HarperCollins Publishers.

Margaret Hillert for "Listen." Used by permission of the author, who controls all rights.

SUN

NO~SWEATER SUN

by Beverly McLoughland

Your arms feel new as growing grass
The first No-Sweater sun,
Your legs feel light as rising air
You *have* to run—
And turn a thousand cartwheels round
And sing—
So dizzy with the giddy sun
Of spring.

THE SUN

by Sandra Liatsos

Someone tossed a pancake,

A buttery, buttery pancake.

Someone tossed a pancake

And flipped it up so high,

That now I see the pancake,

The buttery, buttery pancake,

Now I see that pancake

Stuck against the sky.

11

MISTER SUN

by J. Patrick Lewis

Mister Sun
    Wakes up at dawn,
Puts his golden
    Slippers on,
Climbs the summer
    Sky at noon,
Trading places
    With the moon.

Mister Sun
  Runs away
With the blue tag
  End of day,
Switching off the
  Globe lamplight,
Pulling down the
  Shades of night.

13

ON A SUMMER DAY

by Isabel Joshlin Glaser

Noon's lion-faced sun

shakes out

its orangy mane.

Its tongue

scorches

leaves.

Even the bugs

want

rain.

15

SUN

by Valerie Worth

The sun

Is a leaping fire

Too hot

To go near,

16

But it will still

Lie down

In warm yellow squares

On the floor

Like a flat

Quilt, where

The cat can curl

And purr.

AUGUST

by Sandra Liatsos

The desert sun of August

Is shimmering my street

And turning houses into dunes

That glitter in the heat.

One tree is my oasis.

I need the ice cream man!

His truck comes just as slowly

As a camel caravan.

18

WIND AND CLOUDS

GO WIND

by Lilian Moore

Go wind, blow

Push wind, swoosh.

Shake things

take things

make things

fly.

Ring things

swing things

fling things

high.

Go wind, blow

Push things

wheee.

No, wind, no.

Not me—

not *me.*

21

CLOUDS

by Christina G. Rossetti

White sheep, white sheep,

On a blue hill,

When the wind stops

You all stand still.

When the wind blows

You walk away slow.

White sheep, white sheep,

Where do you go?

FOR KEEPS

by Jean Conder Soule

We had a tug of war today

  Old March Wind and I.

He tried to steal my new red kite

  That Daddy helped me fly.

He huffed and puffed.

   I pulled so hard

And held that string so tight

   Old March Wind gave up at last

And let me keep my kite.

THE MARCH WIND

by Anonymous

I come to work as well as play;

I'll tell you what I do;

I whistle all the livelong day,

"Woo-oo-oo-oo! Woo-oo!"

I toss the branches up and down

　And shake them to and fro;

I whirl the leaves in flocks of brown

　And send them high and low.

I strew the twigs upon the ground;

　The frozen earth I sweep;

I blow the children round and round

　And wake the flowers from sleep.

SPILL

by Judith Thurman

the wind scatters

a flock of sparrows—

a handful of small change

spilled suddenly

from the cloud's pocket.

RAIN AND FOG

TO WALK IN WARM RAIN

by David McCord

To walk in warm rain

    And get wetter and wetter!

To do it again—

To walk in warm rain

    Till you drip like a drain.

To walk in warm rain

    And get wetter and wetter.

GRAYNESS

by Charlotte Zolotow

Fog on the river
fog in the trees
gray mist moving
the golden leaves.

32

Willow bending,

dancelike,

long arms trailing

trancelike.

Gray morning

gray light

gray mist

gray night.

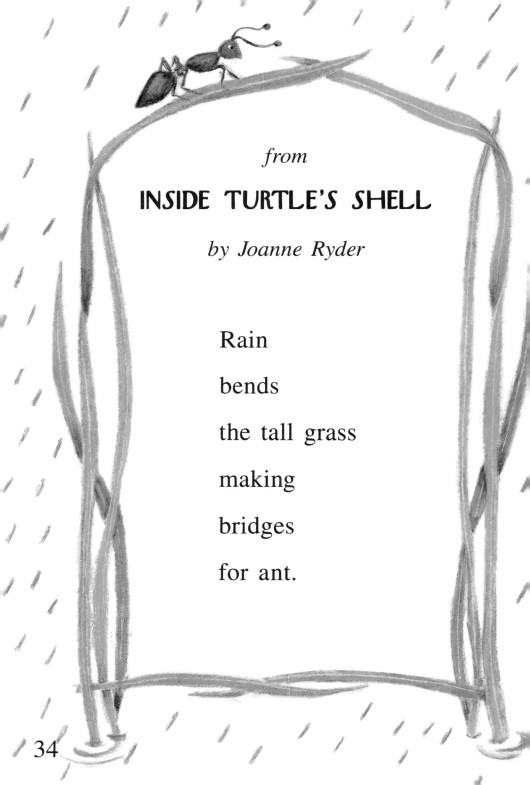

from

INSIDE TURTLE'S SHELL

by Joanne Ryder

Rain

bends

the tall grass

making

bridges

for ant.

RAIN

by Myra Cohn Livingston

Summer rain

is soft and cool,

so I go barefoot

in a pool.

But winter rain

is cold, and pours,

so I must watch it

from indoors.

THUNDER

by Lee Bennett Hopkins

Crashing

      and

Cracking—

Racing

      and

Roaring—

It
whips
through
a cloud.

Why
must
thunder
come
rumbling
this
LOUD?

37

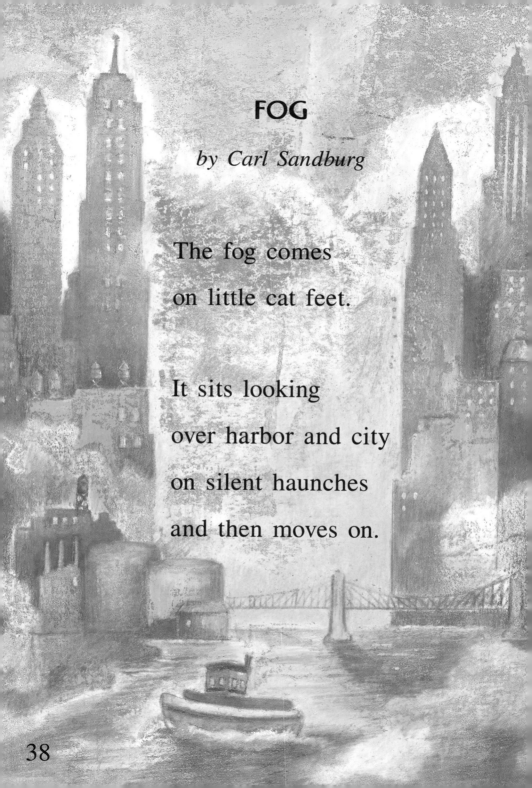

FOG

by Carl Sandburg

The fog comes
on little cat feet.

It sits looking
over harbor and city
on silent haunches
and then moves on.

SNOW AND ICE

LISTEN

by Margaret Hillert

Scrunch, scrunch, scrunch.

Crunch, crunch, crunch.

Frozen snow and brittle ice

Make a winter sound that's nice

Underneath my stamping feet

And the cars along the street.

Scrunch, scrunch, scrunch.

Crunch, crunch, crunch.

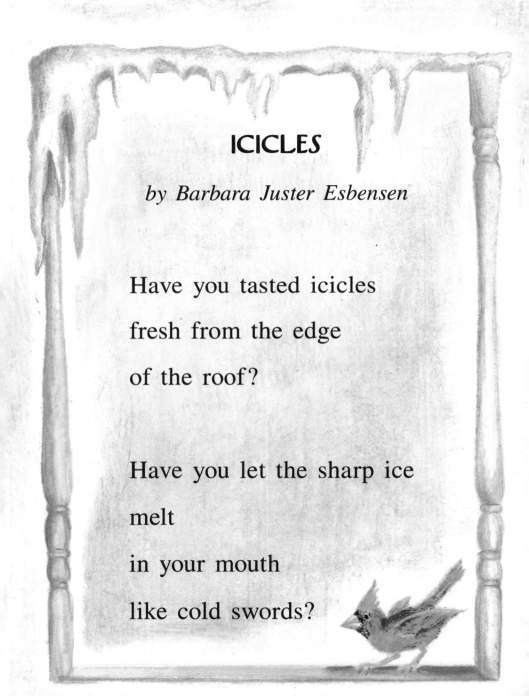

ICICLES

by Barbara Juster Esbensen

Have you tasted icicles

fresh from the edge

of the roof?

Have you let the sharp ice

melt

in your mouth

like cold swords?

The sun plays them
like a glass
xylophone   a crystal
harp.

All day they fall
chiming
into the pockmarked
snow.

LYING ON THINGS

by Dennis Lee

After it snows

I go and lie on things.

I lie on my back

And make snow-angel wings.

I lie on my front

And powder-puff my nose.

I *always* lie on things

Right after it snows.

SNOWFLAKE SOUFFLÉ

by X. J. Kennedy

Snowflake soufflé

Snowflake soufflé

Makes a lip-smacking lunch

On an ice-cold day!

You take seven snowflakes,

You break seven eggs,

And you stir it seven times

With your two hind legs.

Bake it in an igloo,

Throw it on a plate,

And slice off a slice

With a rusty ice-skate.

WINTER MORNING

by Ogden Nash

Winter is the king of showmen,

Turning tree stumps into snow men

And houses into birthday cakes

And spreading sugar over lakes.

Smooth and clean and frosty white

The world looks good enough to bite.

That's the season to be young,

Catching snowflakes on your tongue.

Snow is snowy when it's snowing,

I'm sorry it's slushy when it's going.

WINTER SWEETNESS

by Langston Hughes

This little house is sugar.

Its roof with snow is piled,

And from its tiny window

Peeps a maple-sugar child.

WEATHER TOGETHER

A WEEK OF WEATHER

by Lee Bennett Hopkins

Monday/Muggy-day

Tuesday/Tornado-day

Wednesday/Windy-day

Thursday/Thunder-day

Friday/Foggy-day

Saturday/Soggy-day

Sunday

At last!

SUN

day.

RAIN SONG

by Leland B. Jacobs

Spring rain is pink rain,
   For petals sweet and fair,
Summer rain is rainbow rain,
   With colors everywhere.

The rain of fall is brown rain,
   With leaves that whirl and blow,
And winter rain is white rain,
   But we call it snow.

LOOKING OUT THE WINDOW

by Aileen Fisher

I like it when it shines

on the oaks and pines.

I like it when it snows

and a white wind blows.

I like it when it tinkles

with sprinkles of rain

that crinkle the face

of the windowpane.

UNDERSTANDING

by Myra Cohn Livingston

Sun

and rain

and wind

and storms

and thunder go together.

There has to be a little bit of each

to make the weather.

WEATHER

by Anonymous

Whether the weather be fine,

Or whether the weather be not,

Whether the weather be cold,

Or whether the weather be hot,

We'll weather the weather

Whatever the weather

Whether we like it or not.

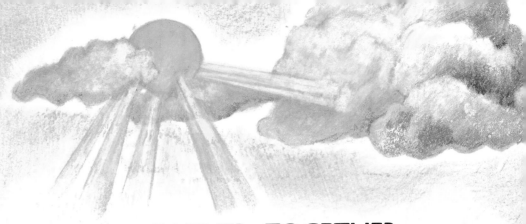

WEATHER TOGETHER

by Lillian M. Fisher

There are holes in the clouds
  where the sun peeks through,
Patches of sky,
  scraps of blue.
It's raining rain
  and bits of ice
Bounce down like
  tiny grains of rice.

This weather together

changes by the minute

And I can hardly wait

to walk out in it!

INDEX OF AUTHORS AND TITLES

Anonymous, 26–27, 59
August, 18

Clouds, 22–23

Esbensen, Barbara Juster, 42–43

Fisher, Aileen, 56
Fisher, Lillian M., 60–61
Fog, 38
For Keeps, 24–25

Glaser, Isabel Joshlin, 14–15
Go Wind, 20–21
Grayness, 32–33

Hillert, Margaret, 40
Hopkins, Lee Bennett, 36–37, 52–53
Hughes, Langston, 50

Icicles, 42–43
Inside Turtle's Shell, from, 34

Jacobs, Leland B., 54

Kennedy, X.J., 46–47

Lee, Dennis, 44–45
Lewis, J. Patrick, 12–13
Liatsos, Sandra, 11, 18
Listen, 40
Livingston, Myra Cohn, 35, 58
Looking Out the Window, 56
Lying on Things, 44–45

March Wind, The, 26–27

McCord, David, 31
McLoughland, Beverly, 10
Mister Sun, 12–13
Moore Lilian, 20–21

Nash, Ogden, 48–49
No-Sweater Sun, 10

On a Summer Day, 14–15

Rain, 35
Rain Song, 54
Rossetti, Christina G., 22–23
Ryder, Joanne, 34

Sandburg, Carl, 38
Soule, Jean Conder, 24–25
Snowflake Soufflé, 46–47
Spill, 28
Sun, 16–17
Sun, The, 11

To Walk in Warm Rain, 31
Thunder, 36–37
Thurman, Judith, 28

Understanding, 58

Weather, 59
Weather Together, 60–61
Week of Weather, A, 52–53
Winter Morning, 48–49
Winter Sweetness, 50
Worth, Valerie, 16–17

Zolotow, Charlotte, 32–33